T0145584

The Life
Truimphant

JAMES ALLEN TITLES

———◦•◦———

The Life
Triumphant

James Allen

MEDIA

Published 2019 by Gildan Media LLC
aka G&D Media
www.GandDmedia.com

Design by Meghan Day Healey of Story Horse, LLC

Library of Congress Cataloging-in-Publication Data is available upon request

ISBN: 978-1-7225-0243-0

10   9   8   7   6   5   4   3   2   1

Contents

Foreword

Every being lives in his own mental world; his joys and sorrows are the creations of his own mind, and are dependent upon the mind for their existence. In the midst of the world, darkened with many sins and many sorrows, in which the majority live, there abides another world, lighted up with shining virtues and unpolluted joy, in which the perfect ones live. This world can be found and entered, and the way to it is by self-control and moral excellence. It is the world of the perfect life, and rightly belongs to man, who is not complete until crowned with perfection. The perfect life is not the far-away, impossible thing that men who are in darkness imagine it to be; it is supremely possible, and very near and real. Man remains a craving, weeping, sinning, repenting creature just so long as he wills to do so by clinging to these weak conditions; but when he wills to shake off his dark dreams and to rise, he arises and achieves.

—James Allen

Faith and
Courage

For those who will fight bravely, and not yield,
there is triumphant victory over all the dark
things of life. I state this at the beginning, that
the reader may know there is no uncertainty about
it; and in the course of this book I shall show what
are the elements, in character and conduct, which
go to build up the life of calm strength and super-
lative victory.

To stand face to face with Truth; to arrive,
after innumerable wanderings and pains, at wisdom and bliss; not to be finally defeated and cast
out, but ultimately to triumph over every inward
foe—such is man's divine destiny, such his glori-

ous goal; and this, every saint, sage, and saviour
has declared.

In the present stage of the life of humanity,
comparatively few reach this place of triumph—
though all will reach it at last—yet there is a glorious company of perfect ones who have attained in
the past, and their number is being added to with
each succeeding age. Men are as yet learners in
the school of life, and most men die learners; but
some there are who, in this life, through fixity of
purpose and strenuous fighting against darkness,
pain, and ignorance, acquire a right knowledge of
life, and pass joyfully beyond the pupil stage. Man
is not to remain *for ever* a schoolboy in the universe, to be whipped for follies and errors; when
he wills and wishes, he can set his mind upon his
task, and master the lessons of life, becoming a
confident and skilled scholar, living in understanding and peace, and not in ignorance and misery.

The sorrows of life are profound and deeply
rooted, but they can be fathomed and rooted out;
the passions and emotions of human nature are, in
their ungoverned state, overwhelming and pain-
fully conflicting, but they can be so softened down,
harmonized, and wisely directed and understood,
as to become obedient servants for the outworking of enlightened purposes. The difficulties of life
are great, its battles fierce, and its wished-for issues

are uncertain and elusive; so much so, that every hour men and women are breaking down under the strain; yet these conditions have no objective and arbitrary existence; in their true nature they are subjective and purely mental, and can be transcended. There is no inherent and permanent evil in the universal order; and the mind can be lifted up to that moral altitude where evil can touch it no more.

A steadfast faith in an Eternal and Universal Justice, in an over-ruling Good, is the prelude to the Life Triumphant. The man who aims to become strong, serene, and steadfast at heart, must, at the outset, have no doubt that the Heart of Life is good. He who is to gaze upon the Cosmic Order, and experience the rapture of emancipation, must realize that there is no disorder in his life but that which he creates. This realization is difficult, so prone is the mind, in its imperfect stages, to self-pity and self-justification, but it can be attained, and must be attained by him who is to live the freed life. At first it must be believed, and the belief must be adhered to until it ripens into realization and knowledge.

The sufferings of life are greatly reduced when they are accepted as disciplinary experiences, and the man of faith does so accept them. The sufferings of life are transcended and put away when all experiences are accounted good, and are utilized in the development of character, and the man of knowledge does so regard and utilize them.

Faith is the grey dawn which precedes the full and perfect day of knowledge. Without it there can be no attainment of strength, no permanent security of heart. The man of faith does not succumb when difficulties present themselves; he does not despair when troubles overtake him. However steep and dark his path may seem, he looks forward to a brighter pathway ahead; sees a destination of rest and light beyond.

They who have no faith in the triumph of good ignominiously succumb to the elements of evil. And this must be so; for he who does not elevate good, elevates evil, and, seeing evil as the master of life, he receives the wages of evil.

There are those who, having yielded to defeat in the battle of life, talk thoughtlessly about the wrongs they have suffered at the hands of others. They believe—and try to make others believe—that they would have been successful, or rich, or famous but for the treachery and villainy of those about them. They tell, for the thousandth time, how they have been deceived, defrauded, and degraded by others. They imagine that they themselves are all trust, all innocence, all honesty and good nature, and that nearly everybody else is all that is bad and malicious. They tell how they would have been just as prosperous and honoured as others if they had been as selfish as those others; and that their great drawback, and the chief source, in themselves, of their failures, is that they were born with too great an endowment of unselfishness. Such self-praising complainers cannot distinguish between good and evil, and their faith in human nature and the goodness of the universe is dead. Looking upon others, they have eyes for evil only; looking upon themselves, they see only suffering innocence. Rather than discover any evil in themselves, they would have all humanity bad. In their hearts they have enthroned the wretched Demon of Evil as the Lord of Life, and see in the course of things only a selfish scramble in which the good is always crushed, and evil rises triumphant. Blind to their own folly and ignorance and weakness, they see nothing but injustice in their fate, nothing but misery and wretchedness in their present condition.

He who would have even a useful and successful life—much more so a spiritually noble and victorious one—must at once root out and cast away this wretched condition of mind that negatives all that is good and pure, and gives the pre-eminence to all that is base and impure. Misfortune, misery and defeat most surely await the man who believes that dishonesty, deceit, and selfishness are the best weapons whereby to achieve a successful life. What courage and strength can a man develop, and what quiet and happiness can he enjoy, who believes that in order to keep pace with others he must continually deny and discourage the better qualities of his nature? The man who believes that evil is more powerful than good, and that bad men have the best of life, is still involved in the elements of evil; and, being so involved, he suffers—must necessarily suffer—defeat.

It may appear to you that the world is given over to wickedness; that the bad prosper, and the good fail; that there is nothing but chance, injustice, and disorder; but do not believe this: regard it as an illusive appearance; conclude that you do not see life as it really is; that you have not yet fathomed the causes of things, and that when you can look upon life through a purer heart and a wiser mind, you will see and understand its equity. And truly when you do so look at life, you will see good where you now see evil, order where now appears disorder, justice where now injustice seems to prevail.

The universe is a cosmos, not a chaos, and the bad do not prosper. It is true there is much evil in the world, otherwise there would be no necessity for moral aims, but there is also much misery in the world, and the evil and misery are related as cause and effect. It is equally true that there is much good in the world, and much abiding gladness, and the good and gladness are related as cause and effect.

He who has acquired that faith in the power and supremacy of good which no apparent injustice, no amount of suffering, and no catastrophe can shake, will pass through all emergencies, all trials and difficulties, with a sublime courage that defies the demons of doubt and despair. He may not succeed in all his plans; he may even encounter much failure; but when he fails, it will be that he may frame nobler purposes and ascend to higher achievements. He will only fail in order to reach a success greater than that of which he at first dreamed. His life will not, cannot, be a failure; some of its details may fail, but this will be but the breaking of weak links in the chain of character and events, in order that the whole may be made more strong and complete.

There is an animal courage which can calmly face the fire of an enemy in battle, or the fierce rage of wild beasts, but which fails in the battle of life, and breaks down when confronted with the beasts that rage within one's own heart. It requires a higher, diviner courage to remain calm in the hour of deprivation and calamity than in the heat of battle, to overcome self than to overcome another. And this diviner courage is the companion of faith.

A mere theological belief (commonly confounded with faith) will not avail. Beliefs about God, Jesus, Creation, etc., are mere surface opinions (derived chiefly from custom) which do not reach down to the real life of a man, and have no power to bestow faith. Such beliefs may accompany faith, but they are distinct from it. Frequently those who hold most tenaciously to particular beliefs about God, Jesus, and the Bible, are most lacking in faith—that is, they give way to complaint, despondency, and grief immediately some petty trouble overtakes them. If one is given to irritability, anxiety, hopelessness, and lamentations over the untoward things of life, let him know that, in spite of his religious belief or metaphysical philosophy, he lacks faith; for where faith is there is courage, there is fortitude, there is steadfastness and strength.

The opinions of men are lightly to be considered, for they are changing with every new breeze of thought. They have very little part in the reality of things, being the bubbles of a surface effervescence; but behind all opinions there is the same human heart. The "godless" are they who are godless, even though they be members of churches and make great profession of faith in God. The "godly" are they who are goodly even though they make no profession of religion, the complainers and bewailers are the faithless and unbelieving. Those who deny or belittle the power of good, and in their lives and actions affirm and magnify the power of evil, are the only real atheists. Faith bestows that sublime courage that rises superior to the petty and selfish disappointments and troubles of life, that acknowledges no defeat except as a step to victory; that is strong to endure, patient to wait, and energetic to struggle; that perceives the benign law to Truth in all things, and is assured of the final triumph of the heart, of the kingly power of the mind.

Light up, then, O man! the lamp of faith in your heart, and walk through the darkness guided by its illuminating rays. Its light is dim, and cannot be compared with the sun-like effulgence of knowledge, but it suffices to lead one safely through the mists of doubt and the black darkness of despair; along the narrow, thorny ways of sickness and sorrow, and over the treacherous places of temptation and uncertainty; it enables him to ward off and outstrip the foul beasts that rage in the jungle of his heart, and to reach safely the open plains of a pure life and the mountain levels of conquest where the dim light of faith is no longer needed, for, leaving behind him all the darkness, all the doubt and error and sorrow, he enters into a new consciousness and upon a higher round of life, and works, acts, and lives self-contained and peaceful, in the full and glorious light of knowledge.

Manliness and Sincerity

efore a man can be truly godly, he must be manly; before a woman can be truly godly, she must be womanly. There can be no true goodness apart from moral strength. Simperings, affectations, flatteries, insincerities and smiling hypocrisies—let these things be for ever destroyed, and banished from our minds. Evil is inherently weak, ineffectual, cowardly. Good is essentially strong, effective, courageous. In teaching men and women to be good, I teach them to be strong, free, self-reliant. They will greatly misunderstand me and the principles which I enunciate who imagine that because I teach gentleness and purity and patience I teach the cultivation of an effeminate weakness. It is only the manly man and womanly woman that can properly understand those divine qualities, and none are better equipped to achieve the Life Triumphant than they who, along with active moral qualities and a high sense of purity and honour, are also possessed of the strong animal nature of the normal man.

That animal force which, in various forms, surges within you, and which, in the hour of excitement, carries you blindly away, causing you to forget your higher nature and to forfeit your manly dignity and honour—that same force controlled, mastered, and rightly directed, will endow you with a divine strength by which you can achieve the highest, noblest, most blissful victories of true living.

The Caliban within you is to be scourged and disciplined into obedience. You are to be master of your heart, your mind, yourself. Man is only weak and abject when he gives up the reins of government to the lower, instead of directing the lower by the higher. Your passions are to be your servants and slaves, not your masters. See that you keep them in their places, duly controlled and commanded, and they shall render you faithful, strong, and happy service.

You are not "vile." There is no part of your body or mind that is vile. Nature does not make mistakes. The universe is framed on Truth. All your functions, faculties, and powers are good, and to direct them rightly is wisdom, holiness, happiness; to direct them wrongly is folly, sin, and misery.

Men waste themselves in excesses; in bad tempers, hatreds, gluttonies, and unworthy and unlawful pleasures, and then blame life. They should blame themselves.

A man should have more self-respect than to abuse his nature in any way. He should command himself always; should avoid excitement and hurry; should be too noble to give way to anger, to resent the actions and opinions of others, or fruitlessly to argue with an abusive and cantankerous assailant.

A quiet, unobtrusive, and unoffending dignity is the chief mark of a ripe and perfect manhood. Honour others and respect yourself. Choose your own path and walk it with a firm, unflinching step, but avoid a meddlesome interference with others. In the true man opposing qualities are blended and harmonized; a yielding kindness accompanies an unbending strength. He adapts himself gently and wisely to others without sacrificing the steadfast principles upon which his manhood is built. To have that iron strength that can go calmly to death rather than yield one jot of truth, along with that tender sympathy that can shield the weak and mistaken enemy, is to be manly with a divine manhood.

Be true to the dictates of your own conscience, and respect all who do the same, even though their conscience should lead them in a direction the reverse of your own. One of the most unmanly tendencies is to pity another because he chooses opinions or religion contrary to those of one's self. Why pity a man because he is an Agnostic, or an Atheist, or a Buddhist, or a Christian? Because he does not hold this opinion or that belief? Such pity would be rightly named contempt. It is the office of pity to feel for the weak, the afflicted, and the helpless. Pity never says "I pity you;" it does kind deeds. It is superciliousness that professes pity for the strong, the self-reliant, for those who have the courage to mark out their own path and to walk it boldly. Why should he perforce hold my opinion or yours? If what I say and do appeal to his reason and conscience as right, then he will be one with me and will work hand in hand with me. But if my work be not his work, he is none the less a man. He has his duty, though it be not my duty. When I meet one who is self-respecting, and who dares to think for himself, I will salute him as a man, and not harbour in my heart a contemptible pity for him, because, forsooth, he rejects my conclusions.

If we are to be responsible, self-acting beings in a law-begirt universe, let us be masters of our own wills, and respect the free-will of others; if we are to be strong and manly, let us be large-hearted and magnanimous; if we are to triumph over the miseries of life, let us rise superior to the pettiness of our nature.

Men weep in their weakness, and cry out in misery of heart and degradation of mind. How plain, then, is the way of emancipation; how sublime the task of triumph! be master of yourself. Eliminate weakness. Exorcise the mocking fiend, selfishness, in whom is all weakness and wretchedness. Do not pander to effeminate and unnatural cravings, to unlawful desires, or to morbid self-love and self-pity; give them no quarter, but promptly stamp them out with disciplinary decision and strength. A man should hold himself, as it were, in the hollow of his hand. He should be able to take up and to lay down. He should know how to use things, and not be used by them. He should neither be the helpless captive of luxury nor the whipped slave of want, but should be self-contained and self-sufficient, master of himself under all conditions. He must train and direct his will in the way of self-mastery which is the way of obedience—obedience to the law of his nature. Disobedience to law is the supreme evil in man, the source of all his sin and sorrow. In his ignorance he imagines he can triumph over law and subdue the wills of others. He thus destroys his power. Man can triumph over his disobedience, over ignorance, sin, egotism, and lawlessness, he can conquer self; and herein lies his manly strength and divine power. He can comprehend the law of his being, and obey it as a child understands and obeys the will of its father. He can sit the crowned king of all his functions and faculties, using them wisely in unselfish service, and not as instruments of selfishness and greed. There is no bad habit that he cannot uproot, no sin that he cannot subdue, no sorrow that he cannot comprehend and conquer. "Let a man then know his worth, and keep things under his feet. Let him not peep or steal, or skulk up and down with the air of a charity-boy, or a bastard, or an interloper, in the world which exists for him."

A manly self-reliance is not only compatible with, but is the accompaniment of, a divine humility. A man is only arrogant and egotistic when he usurps authority over others. He cannot claim nor exercise too great an authority over himself. Strong self-command with gentle consideration for others, combine to make the truly manly man.

To begin with, a man must be honest, upright, sincere. Deceit is the blindest folly. Hypocrisy is the weakest thing on earth. In trying to deceive others, a man most of all deceives himself. A man should be so free from guile, meanness, and deceit as to be able to look everybody in the face with a clear, open, unflinching gaze, free from shame and confusion, and with no inward shrinking or misgivings. Without sincerity a man is but a hollow mask, and whatsoever work he attempts to do, it will be lifeless and ineffectual. Out of a hollow vessel nothing but the sound of hollowness can come; and from insincerity nothing but empty words can proceed.

Many who are not consciously hypocrites, yet fall victims, thoughtlessly, to little insincerities which undermine happiness and destroy the moral fabric of their character. Some of these people go regularly to their place of worship: they pray daily, year after year, for a purer heart and life, yet come from their devotions to vilify an enemy, or, worse still, to ridicule or slander an absent friend for whom, when they meet him, or her, they will have nothing but smiles and smooth words. The pitiful part of it is that they are totally unconscious of their insincerity, and when their friends desert them, they speak complainingly of the faithlessness and hollowness of the world, and of people generally, and tell you sadly that there are no true friends in this world.

Truly, for such there are no abiding friendships, for insincerity, even if not seen, is felt, and those who are incapable of bestowing trust and truth, cannot receive it. Be true to others, and others will be true to you. Think well of an enemy, and defend the absent friend. If you have lost faith in human nature, discover where you have gone wrong yourself.

In the Confucian code of morals sincerity is one of the "Five Great Virtues," and Confucius thus speaks of it: "It is sincerity which places a crown upon our lives; without it, our best actions would be valueless; the seeming virtuous, mere hypocrites; and the shining light, which dazzles us with its splendors, but a poor passing gleam ready to be extinguished by the slightest breath of passion. . . . To be pure in mind, you must be free from self-deception—you must hate vice, as you would a disagreeable odor, and love virtue, as you would some beautiful object. There can be no self-respect without it, and this is why the superior man must be guarded in his hours of solitude.

"The worthless man secretly employs his idle moments in vicious acts, and there is no limit to his wickedness. In the presence of the pure he plays the hypocrite, and puts forward none but his good qualities; yet how does this dissembling avail him when his true character is revealed to the first scrutinizing glance?

"It has been said that there is a strict watch kept over that which is pointed at by many hands, and gazed at by many eyes; it is in solitude, then, that the upright man has the greatest reason to be most guarded."

Thus the sincere man does not do or say that which he would be ashamed of were it brought to light. His uprightness of spirit enables him to walk upright and confident among his fellow-men. His presence is a strong protection, and his words are direct and powerful because they are true. Whatever may be his work, it prospers. Though he may not always please the ears of men, he wins their hearts; they rely on him, trust and honour him.

Courage, self-reliance, sincerity, generosity and kindness—these are the virtues which constitute a robust manhood; without them, a man is but clay in the hands of circumstances; a weak, wavering thing that cannot rise into the freedom and joy of a true life. Every young man should cultivate and foster these virtues, and as he succeeds in living them, will he prepare himself to achieve the Life Triumphant.

I see coming upon the earth a new race of men and women—men who will be men indeed strong, upright, noble; too wise to stoop to anger, uncleanness, strife and hatred—women who will be women indeed, gentle, truthful, pure; too pitying to stoop to gossip, slander and deception; and from their loins will proceed superior beings of the same noble type; and the dark fiends of error and evil will fall back at their approach; they will regenerate the earth; they will dignify man, and vindicate nature, restoring humanity to love, happiness, and peace; and the life of victory over sin and sorrow will be established in the earth.

Energy
and Power

How wonderful is the universal energy! Never-tiring, inexhaustible, and apparently eternal in its operation, it moves in atom and in star, informing the fleeting shapes of time with its restless, glowing, pulsating power.

Man is a portion of this creative energy, and in him it manifests, through a combination of mental faculties, as affection, passion, intelligence, morality, reason, understanding, and wisdom. He is not merely a blind conductor of energy, but he consciously uses, controls, and directs it. Slowly, but with certainty, is he gaining control of the forces without, and is making them do him obedient service; and just as surely will he gain control of the forces within—the subtle energies of thought—and direct them into channels of harmony and happiness.

Man's true place in the Cosmos is that of a king, not a slave, a commander under the Law of Good, and not a helpless tool in the reign of Evil. His own body and mind are the dual dominion over which he is to reign, a Lord of Truth, the master of himself, the wise user and controller of his store of pure, eternal, creative energy. Let him walk the earth unashamed, strong, valiant, tender, and benign; no longer prostrate in self-abasement, but walking erect in the dignity of perfect manhood; not groveling in selfishness and remorse, and crying for pardon and mercy, but standing firm and free in the sublime majesty of a sinless life.

Long has man regarded himself as vile, and weak, and unworthy, and has been content to remain so; but in the new era which has just now burst upon the world, he is to make the glorious discovery that he is pure, and powerful, and noble when he rises up and wills; and the rising up is not against any outward enemy; not against neighbour, nor governments, nor laws, nor spirits, nor principalities, nor powers, but against the ignorance, folly, and misery which beset him in the dominion of his own mind. For it is only by ignorance and folly that man is slavish; by knowledge and wisdom his kingship is restored.

Let them who will, preach man's weakness and helplessness, but I will teach his strength and power. I write for men, not for babes; for those who are eager to learn, and earnest to achieve; for those who will put away (for the world's good) a petty personal indulgence, a selfish desire, a mean thought, and live on as though it were not, sans craving and regret. The Truth is not for the frivolous and the thoughtless; the Life Triumphant is not for triflers and loiterers.

Man is a master. If he were not, he could not act contrary to law. Thus his so-called weakness is an indication of strength; his sin is the inversion of his capacity for holiness. For what is his weakness and sin but misdirected energy, misapplied power? In this sense, the wrong-doer is strong, not weak; but he is ignorant and exerts his strength in wrong directions instead of right, against the law of things instead of with it. Suffering is the recoil of misdirected strength. The bad man becomes good by reversing his conduct. If you are weeping over your sins, cease to commit those sins, and establish yourself in their opposing virtues. It is thus that weakness is converted into strength, helplessness into power, and suffering into bliss. By turning his energies from the old channels of vice, and directing them into the new channels of virtue, the sinner becomes the saint.

While the universal energy may be unlimited, in particular forms its sum it strictly limited. A man is possessed of a given amount of energy, and he can use or misuse it, can conserve and concentrate it, or dissipate and disperse it. Power is concentrated energy; wisdom is that energy adapted to beneficent ends. He is the man of influence and power who directs all his energies toward one great purpose, and patiently works and waits for its fulfillment, sacrificing his desires in other and more pleasant directions. He is the man of folly and weakness who, thinking chiefly of pleasure, gratifies the desire of the hour, or follows the whim and impulse of the moment, and so drifts thoughtlessly into peevishness and poverty of mind.

The energy used in one direction is not available for use in other directions; this is a universal law both in mind and matter. Emerson calls it "the law of compensation." Gain in a given direction necessitates loss in its opposite direction. The force placed in one scale is deducted from the other scale. Nature is always endeavoring to strike a balance. The energy which is dissipated in idleness is not given to work. The pleasure-seeker cannot also be the Truth-seeker. The force wasted in a fit of bad temper is drawn from the man's store of virtue, particularly the virtue of patience. Spiritually, this law of compensation is the law of sacrifice. Selfish pleasure must be sacrificed if purity is to be gained; hatred must be yielded up if love is to be acquired; vice must be renounced if virtue is to be embraced.

Earnest men soon discover that if they are to accomplish anything that is successful, strong, and enduring, either is worldly, intellectual, or spiritual channels, they must curb their desires, and sacrifice much that seems sweet; yea, even much that seems important. Hobbies, bodily and mental indulgences, enticing companionships, alluring pleasures, and all work that does not tend to some central purpose in his life, must be sacrificed by the man of strong resolve. He opens his eyes to the fact that time and energy are strictly limited, and so he economizes the one and concentrates the other.

Foolish men waste their energies in swinish ease and gluttonous indulgence, in frivolous pleasures and empty talk; in hateful thoughts and irritable outbursts of passion; in vain controversy and meddlesome interference; and then complain that many are more "fortunately" equipped than they are for a useful, successful, or great life, and they envy their honoured neighbour who has sacrificed self to duty, and has devoted all his energies to the faithful performance of the business of his life. "He who is just, speaks the truth, and does what is his own business, him the world will hold dear." Let a man attend to his own business, consecrating all his faculties to, and concentrating all his energies upon, the perfect accomplishment of the task of his life, not stepping aside to condemn or interfere with the duties of others, and he will find life simple, strong, and happy.

The universe is girt with goodness and strength, and it protects the good and the strong. Evil and weakness are self-destructive. Dissipation is annihilation. All nature loves strength. I see no inherent cruelty in "the survival of the fittest." It is a spiritual as well as a natural law. The stronger qualities in the beast are the fittest to evolve a higher type. The nobler moral qualities in man are his emancipators, and it is well that they should dominate and ultimately crush out the ignoble tendencies. Most certain it is that he who gives dominion to the lower, courts destruction, and does not survive, either in the struggle of life without or the battle of Truth within. The life given to the lower is lost to the higher; yea, it is finally lost also to the lower, and so all is lost, for evil is ultimately nothingness. But the life given to the higher is preserved, and is not lost to anything, for, while it sacrifices much that the world holds precious, it does not sacrifice anything that is precious in reality. The untrue and worthless must perish, and he who consecrates himself to the good and the true is content that they should perish, and so at last he stands where sacrifice ends, and all is gain—such a one survives in the struggle of life without, and he conquers in the battle of Truth within.

First, then, he strong. Strength is the firm basis on which is built the temple of the Triumphant Life. Without a central motive and fixed resolve, your life will be a poor, weak drifting, unstable thing. Let the act of the moment be governed by the deep abiding purpose of the heart. You will act differently at different times, but the act will not be wrong if the heart is right. You may fall and go astray at times, especially under great stress, but you will quickly regain yourself, and will grow wiser and stronger thereby so long as you guide yourself by the moral compass within, and do not throw it away to gratify effeminate indulgence and give yourself up to uncertain drifting. Follow your conscience. Be true to your convictions. Do at the moment what you regard as right, and put away all procrastination, vacillation, and fear. If you are convinced that in the performance of your duty under certain circumstances the severest measures are necessary, carry out those measures, and let there be no uncertainty about it. Err on the side of strength rather than weakness. The measures you adopt may not be the best, but if they are the best your know, then your plain duty is to carry them out; by so doing you will discover the better way, if you are anxious for progress, and are willing to learn. Deliberate beforehand, but in the time for action do not hesitate. Avoid anger and stubbornness, lust and greed. The angry man is the weak man. The stubborn man, who refuses to learn or mend his ways, is the foolish man. He grows old in folly, and gray hairs do not bring him reverence or honour. The sensualist has energy for pleasure only, and reserves none for manliness and self-respect. The greedy man is blind to the nobility of human nature and the glory of a true life; he spends his energies in perpetuating the miseries of hell, instead of enjoying the happiness of heaven.

Your strength is with you, and you can spend it in burrowing downward or in climbing upward. You can dissipate it in selfishness or conserve it in goodness. The same energy will enable you to become a beast or a god. The course along which you direct it will determine its effect. Do not think the thought, "My mind is weak," but convert weakness into strength, and energy into power by redirecting your mental forces. Turn your thoughts into noble channels. Put away vain longings and foolish regrets; abolish complaint and self-condolence, and have no dalliance with evil. Lift your face upward. Rise up in your divine strength, and spurn from your mind and life all meanness and weakness. Do not live the false life of a pulling slave, but live the true life of a conquering master.

Self-Control and Happiness

When mental energy is allowed to follow the line of least resistance, and to fall into easy channels, it is called weakness; when it is gathered, focused, and forced into upward and difficult directions, it becomes power; and this concentration of energy and acquisition of power is brought about by means of self-control.

In speaking of self-control, one is easily misunderstood. It should not be associated with a destructive repression, but with a constructive expression. The process is not one of death, but of life; it is a divine and masterly transmutation in which the weak in converted into the strong, the coarse into the fine, and the base into the noble; in which virtue takes the place of vice, and dark passion is lost in bright intellectuality.

The man who merely smothers up and hides away his real nature without any higher object in view than to create a good impression upon others concerning his character, is practising hypocrisy, and not self-control. As the mechanic transmutes coal into gas, and water into steam, and then concentrates and utilizes the finer forces thus generated for the comfort and convenience of men, so the man who intelligently practises self-control transmutes his lower inclinations into the finer qualities of intelligence and morality to the increase, of his own and the world's happiness.

A man is happy, wise, and great in the measure that he controls himself; he is wretched, foolish, and mean in the measure that he allows his animal nature to dominate his thoughts and actions.

He who controls himself, controls his life, his circumstances, his destiny; and wherever he goes he carries his happiness with him as an abiding possession. He who does not control himself, is controlled by his passions, by his circumstances, and by his fate; and if he cannot gratify the desire of the moment, he is disappointed and miserable. He depends for his fitful happiness on external things.

There is no force in the universe which can be annihilated or lost. Energy is transformed, but not destroyed. To shut the door upon old and bad habits is to open it to new and better ones. Renunciation precedes regeneration. Every self-indulgence, every forbidden pleasure, every hateful thought renounced is transformed into something more purely and permanently beautiful. Where debilitating excitements are cut off, there spring up rejuvenating joys. The seed dies that the flower may appear; the grub perishes, but the dragon-fly comes forth.

Truly, the transformation is not instantaneous; nor is the transition a pleasant and painless process. Nature demands effort and patience as the price of growth. In the march of progress, every victory is contested with struggle and pain; but the victory is achieved, and it abides. The struggle passes; the pain is temporary only. To demolish a firmly fixed habit, to break up a mental tendency that has become automatic with long use, and to force into birth and growth a fine characteristic or lofty virtue—to accomplish this necessitates a painful metamorphosis, a transitional period of darkness, to pass through which, patience and endurance are required: and this is where men fail; this is where they slip back into their old, easy,

animal ruts, and abandon self-control as too strenuous and severe. Thus they fall short of permanent
happiness, and the life of triumph over evil is hidden from their eyes.

The permanent happiness which men seek
in dissipation, excitement, and abandonment to
unworthy pleasures is found only in the life which
reverses all this—the life of self-control. So far as
a man deviates from perfect self-command, just
so far does he fall short of perfect happiness, and
sink into misery and weakness, the lowest limit
of which is madness, entire lack of mental control, the condition of irresponsibility. In so far as
a man approximates to perfect self-command, just
so near does he approach to perfect happiness, and
rise into joy and strength; and so glorious are the
possibilities of such divine manhood, that no limit
can be set to its grandeur and bliss.

If a man will understand how intimately, yea,
how inseparably, self-control and happiness are
associated, he has but to look into his own heart,
and upon the world around, to find there the
joy destroying effects of uncontrolled tendencies.
Looking upon the lives of men and women, he will
perceive how the hasty word, the bitter retort, the
act of deception, the blind prejudice and foolish
resentment bring wretchedness and even ruin in
their train. Looking into his own life, what days

of consuming remorse, of restless anxiety, and of crushing sorrow rise up before his mind—periods of intense suffering through which he has passed through lack of self-control.

But in the right life, the well-governed life, the victorious life, all these things pass away. New conditions obtain, and purer, more espiritual instruments are employed for the achievements of happy ends. There is no more remorse, because there is no more wrong-doing; there is no more anxiety, because there is no more selfishness; there is no more sorrow, because Truth is the source of action.

That much-desired thing which self pursues with breathless and uncontrolled eagerness, yet fails to overtake, comes unbidden, and begs to be admitted, to him who works and waits in perfect self-command. Hatred, impatience, greed, self-indulgence, vain ambitions, and blind desires—the instruments by which self shapes its ill-finished existence, what clumsy tools they are, and how ignorant and unskillful are they who employ them! Love, patience, kindness, self-discipline, transmuted ambitions and chastened desires—instruments of Truth, by which is shaped a well-finished existence, what perfect tools they are, and how wise and skillful are they who use them!

Whatsoever is gained by feverish haste and selfish desire, is attained in fuller measure by quietness and renunciation. Nature will not be hastened. She brings all to perfection in due season. Truth will not be commanded. He has his conditions, and must be obeyed. Than haste and anger nothing is more superfluous. A man has to learn that he cannot command things, but that he can command himself; that he cannot coerce the wills of others, but that he can mold and master his own will: and things serve him who serves Truth; people seek guidance of him who is master of himself.

It is a little understood, yet simple and profound truth, that the man who cannot command himself under the severest external stress, is unfit to guide others or to control affairs. It is the fundamental principle in the moral and political teaching of Confucius that, before attempting to govern affairs, a man should learn to govern himself. Men who habitually give way, under pressure, to hysterical suspicions, outbursts of resentment, and explosions of anger, are unfit for weighty responsibilities and lofty duties, and usually fail, sooner or later, even in the ordinary duties of life, such as the management of their own family or business. Lack of self-control is foolishness, and folly cannot take precedence of wisdom.

He who is learning how to subdue and control his turbulent, wandering thoughts, is becoming wiser every day; and though for a time the Temple of Joy will not be completed, he will gather strength in laying its foundations and building up its walls; and the day will come when, like a wise master-builder, he will rest at peace in the beautiful habitation which he has built. Wisdom inheres in self-control, and in wisdom is "pleasantness and peace."

The life of self-control is no barren deprivation, no wilderness of monotony. Renunciation there is, but it is the renunciation of the ephemeral and false in order that the abiding and true may be realized. Enjoyment is not cut off; it is intensified. Enjoyment is life; it is the slavish desire for it that kills. Is there anywhere a more miserable man than he who is always longing for some new sensation? Is there anywhere a more blessed being than he who, by self-control, is satisfied, calm, and enlightened? Who has most of physical life and joy—the glutton, the drunkard, and the sensualist who lives for pleasure only, or the temperate man who holds his body in subjection, considering its needs and obeying its uses? I was once eating a ripe, juicy apple as it came from the tree, and a man near me said, "I would give anything if I could enjoy an apple like that." I asked, "Why can't you?" His answer was, "I have drunk whisky and smoked tobacco until I have lost all enjoyment in such things." In pursuit of elusive enjoyments, men lose the abiding joys of life.

And as he who controls his senses has most of physical life, and joy, and strength so he who controls his thoughts has most of spiritual life, and bliss, and power; for not only happiness, but knowledge and wisdom also are revealed by self-control. As the avenues of ignorance and selfishness are closed, the open gates of knowledge and enlightenment appear. Virtue attained is knowledge gained. The pure mind is the enlightened mind. He has well-being who controls himself well.

I hear men speak of the "monotony of goodness." If longing for things in the spirit which one has given up in the letter were "goodness," then indeed would it be monotonous. The man of self-control does not merely give up his base pleasures, he abandons all longing for them. He presses forward, and does not look back; and fresh beauties, new glories, sublimer vistas await him at every step.

I am astonished at the revelations which lie hidden in self-control; I am captivated by the Infinite variety of Truth; I am filled, with joy at the grandeur of the prospect; I am gladdened by its splendor and its peace.

Along the way of self-control there is the joy of victory; the consciousness of expanding and increasing power; the acquisition of the imperishable riches of divine knowledge; and the abiding bliss of service to humankind. Even he who travels only a portion of the way will develop a strength, achieve a success, and experience a joy which the idle and the thoughtless cannot know; and he who goes all the way will become a spiritual conqueror; he will triumph over all evil, and will blot it out; he will gaze with enrapt vision upon the majesty of the Cosmic Order, and will enjoy the immortality of Truth.

Simplicity
and Freedom

You have known what it is to be physically encumbered by some superfluous load; you have experienced the happy relief of dispensing with such load. Your experience illustrates the difference between a life burdened with a complexity of desires, beliefs, and speculations, and one rendered simple and free by the satisfaction of its natural needs, and a calm contemplation of the facts of existence, eliminating all argument and speculation.

There are those who cumber their drawers, cupboards, and rooms with rubbish and lumber. To such an extent is this carried sometimes, that the house cannot be properly cleaned, and vermin swarms. There is no use for the rubbish, but they will not part with it, even though, by so doing, they would also get rid of the vermin; but they like to think that it is there; like to feel that they have *got* it, especially if they are convinced that nobody else has its like; or they reason that it may be of some use some day; or it may become valuable; or it brings up old associations which they occasionally resuscitate, and take a paradoxical pleasure in sorrowing over.

In a sweet, methodical, well-managed house, such superfluities, bringing with them dirt, discomfort, and care, are not allowed to accumulate; or should they have accumulated, they are gathered up and consigned to the fire and the dust-bin, when it is decided to cleanse and restore the house, and give it light, comfort and freedom.

In like manner men hoard up in their minds mental rubbish and lumber, and cling tenaciously to it, and fear its loss. Insatiate desires; thirsty cravings for unlawful and unnatural pleasures; conflicting beliefs about miracles, gods, angels, demons, and interminable theological complexities, hypothesis is piled upon hypothesis, speculation is added to speculation, until the simple, beautiful, all sufficient facts of life are lost to sight and knowledge beneath the metaphysical pile.

Simplicity consists in being rid of this painful confusion of desires and superfluity of opinions, and adhering only to that which is permanent and essential.

And what is permanent in life? What is essential? Virtue alone is permanent; character is essential. So simple is life when it is freed from all superfluities and rightly understood and lived, that it can be reduced to a few unmistakable, easy-to-be-understood, though hard-to-practice principles; and all great minds have so simplified life. Buddha reduced it to eight virtues, in, the practice of which he declared that men would acquire perfect enlightenment; and these eight virtues he reduced to one, which he called *Compassion.* Confucius taught that the perfection of knowledge was contained in five virtues, and these he expressed in one which he called *Reciprocity, or Sympathy.* Jesus reduced the whole of life to the principle of *Love.* Compassion, Sympathy, Love, these three are identical. How simple they are, too! yet I cannot find a man who fully understands the depths and heights of these virtues, for who so fully understood them would embody them in practice. He would be complete, perfect, divine. There would be nothing lacking in him of knowledge and virtue and wisdom. It is only when a man sets earnestly to work to order his life in accordance with the simple precepts of virtue, that he discovers what piles of mental rubbish he has hoarded up, and which he is now compelled to throw away. The exactions, too, which such a course of conduct makes upon his faith, endurance, patience, kindness, humility, reason, and strength of will, are, until the mind approaches the necessary condition of purity and simplicity, painful in their severity. The clearing-out process, whether of one's mind, home, or place of business, is not a light and easy one, but it ends in comfort and repose.

All complexities of detail, whether in things material or mental, are reducible to a few fundamental laws or principles by virtue of which they exist and are regulated. Wise men govern their lives by a few simple rules. A life governed by the central principle of love will be found to be divinely consistent in all its details. Every thought, word, act, will fall into its proper place, and there will be no conflict and confusion.

"What," asked the learned man of the Buddhist saint who had acquired a wide reputation for sanctity and wisdom—"what is the most fundamental thing in Buddhism?" The saint replied, "The most fundamental thing in Buddhism is to cease from evil and to learn to do good." "I did not ask you," said the learned man, "to tell me what every child of three knows; I want you to tell me what is the

most profound, the most subtle, the most important thing in Buddhism." "The most profound, the
most subtle, the most important thing in Buddhism," said the saint, "is to cease from evil and
to learn to do well. It is true that a child of three
may know it, but grey-haired old men fail to put it
into practice." The commentator then goes on to
say that the learned man did not want facts; he
did not want Truth; he wanted to be given some
subtle metaphysical speculation which would give
rise to another speculation, and then to another
and another, and so afford him an opportunity of
bringing into play the wonderful intellect of which
he was so proud.

A member of a philosophical school once
proudly said to me, "Our system of metaphysics is
the most perfect and complicated in the world." I
discovered how complicated it was by becoming
involved in it and then pursuing the process of
extrication back to the facts of life, to simplicity
and freedom. I have since learned how better to
utilize my energy and occupy my time in the pursuit and practice of those virtues that are firm and
sure, rather than to waste it in the spinning of the
pretty but unsubstantial threads of metaphysical
cobwebs.

But while discountenancing assumption and
pride, and that vanity which mistakes its own

hypothesis for reality, I set no premium on ignorance and stupidity. Learning is a good thing. As
an end in itself, as a possession to be proud of, it
is a dead thing; but as a means to the high ends of
human progress and human good it becomes a living power. Accompanied with a lowly mind, it is a
powerful instrument for good. The Buddhist saint
was no less learned than his proud questioner, but
he was more simple and wise. Even hypotheses
will not lead us astray if they are perceived as mere
hypotheses and are not confounded with facts. Yet
the wisest men dispense with all hypotheses, and
fall back on the simple practice of virtue. They thus
become divine, and arrive at the acme of simplicity, enlightenment, and emancipation.

To arrive at the freedom and joy of simplicity,
one must not think less, he must think more; only
the thinking must be set to a high and useful purpose, and must be concentrated upon the facts and
duties of life, instead of dissipated in unprofitable
theorizing.

A life of simplicity is simple in all its parts
because the heart which governs it has become
pure and strong; because it is centered and rested
in Truth. Harmful luxuries in food, and vain superfluities in dress; exaggerations of speech and insincerities of action; thoughts that tend to intellectual
display and empty speculation—all these are set

aside in order that virtue may be better understood and more earnestly embraced; the duties of
life are undertaken in a spirit from which self is
eliminated, and they become transfigured with a
new and glorious light, even the light of Truth; the
great fundamental facts of life, heretofore hidden
from knowledge, and plainly revealed, and the
Eternal Verities about which the wordy theorizers
can only guess and argue, become substantial possessions.

The simple-hearted, the true-hearted, the virtuous and wise, are no longer troubled with doubts
and fears about the future and the unknown and
unknowable. They take their stand upon the duty
of the hour, and on the known and the knowable.
They do not barter away the actual for the hypo-
thetical. They find in virtue an abiding security;
they find in Truth an illuminating light which,
while it reveals to them the true order of the facts
of life, throws a halo of divine promise about the
abyss of the unknown; and so they are at rest.

Simplicity works untrammelled, and becomes
greatness and power. Suspicions, deceptions, impurities, despondencies, bewailings, doubts, and
fears—all these things are cast away, left behind and
ignored, and the freed man, strong, self-possessed,
calm and pure, works in unclouded assurance, and
inhabits heavenly places.

Right-Thinking
and Repose

L ife is a combination of habits, some baneful, some beneficent, all of which take their rise in the one habit of thinking. The thought makes the man, therefore right-thinking is the most important thing in life. The essential difference between a wise man and a fool is that the wise man controls his thinking, the fool is controlled by it. A wise man, determines how and what he shall think, and does not allow external things to divert his thought from the main purpose; but a fool is carried captive by every tyrant thought as it is aroused within him by external things, and he goes through life the helpless tool of impulse, whim, and passion.

Careless, slovenly thinking, commonly called thoughtlessness, is the companion of failure, wrong-doing, and wretchedness. Nothing, no prayers, no religious ceremonies, not even acts of charity, can make up for wrong thinking. Only right-thinking can rectify a wrong life. Only the right attitude of mind toward men and things can bring repose and peace.

The Triumphant Life is only for him whose heart and intellect are attuned to lofty virtue. He must make his thought logical, sequential, harmonious, symmetrical. He must mould and shape his thinking to fixed principles, and thereby establish his life on the sure foundation of knowledge. He must not merely be kind, he must be intelligently kind; must know why he is kind. His kindness must be an invariable quality, and not an intermittent impulse interspersed with fits of resentment and acts of harshness. He must not merely be virtuous under virtuous circumstances; his virtue must be of that kind that shall continue to shine with unabated light when he is assailed with vicious circumstances. He must not allow himself to be hurled from the throne of divine manhood by the shocks of fate or the praise and blame of those about him. Virtue must be his abiding habitation; his refuge from the whirlwind and the storm.

And virtue is not only of the heart; it is of the intellect also; and without this virtue of the intellect, the virtue of the heart is imperilled. Reason, like passion, has its vices. Metaphysical speculations are the riot of the intellect, as sensuality is the riot of the affections. The highest flights of speculation—pleasing as they are—reveal no place of rest, and the strained mind must return to facts and moral principles to find that truth which it seeks. As the soaring bird returns for refuge and rest to its nest in the rock, so must the speculative thinker return to the rock of virtue for surety and peace.

The intellect must be trained to comprehend the principles of virtue, and to understand all that is involved in their practice. Its energies must be restrained from wasteful indulgence in vain subtleties, and be directed in the path of righteousness and the way of wisdom. The thinker must distinguish, in his own mind, between reality and assumption. He must discover the extent of his actual knowledge. He must know what he knows. He must also know what he does not know. He must learn to discriminate between facts and opinions about facts, between belief and knowledge, error and Truth In his search for the right attitude of mind which perceives truth, and works out a wise and radiant life, he must be more logical than logic, more merciless in exposing the errors of his own mind than the most sarcastic logician is in exposing the errors of the minds of others. After pursuing this course of discrimination for a short time, he will be astonished to find how small is the extent of his actual knowledge; yet he will be gladdened by its possession, for small as it is, it is the pure gold of knowledge; and what is better, to have a few grains of gold hidden away in tons of ore, where it is useless, or to extract the gold and throw away the ore? As the miner sifts away bushels of dull earth to find the sparkling diamond, so the spiritual miner, the true thinker, sifts away from his mind the accumulation of opinions, beliefs, speculations, and assumptions to find the bright jewel of Truth which bestows upon its possessor wisdom and enlightenment.

And the concentrated knowledge which is ultimately brought to light by this sifting process is found to be so closely akin to virtue that it cannot be divided from it, cannot be set apart as something different. In his search for knowledge. Socrates discovered virtue. The divine maxims of the Great Teachers are maxims of virtue. When knowledge is separated from virtue, wisdom is lost. What a man practises, that he knows. What he does not practice, that he does not know. A man may write treatises or preach sermons on Love, but if he treat his family harshly, or think spitefully of his enemy, what knowledge has he concerning Love? In the heart of the man of knowledge there dwells a silent and abiding compassion that shames the fine words of the noisy theorist. He only knows what peace is whose heart is free from hatred; who lives at peace with all. Cunning definitions of virtue only serve to deepen ignorance when they proceed from vice-stained lips. Knowledge has a deeper source than the mere memorizing of information. That knowledge is divine which proceeds from acquaintance with virtue. The humility which purges the intellect of its empty opinions and vain assumptions, also fortifies it with a searching insight and invincible power. There is a divine logic which is in-distinguished from love. The reply, "He that is without sin among you, let him first cast a stone at her," is unanswerable logic; it is also perfect love.

The wrong-thinker is known by his vices; the right-thinker is known by his virtues. Troubles and unrest assail the mind of the wrong-thinker, and he experiences no abiding repose. He imagines that others can injure, snub, cheat, degrade and ruin him. Knowing nothing of the protection of virtue, be seeks the protection of self, and takes refuge in suspicion, spite, resentment, and retaliation, and is burnt in the fire of his own vices. When slandered, he slanders in return; when accused, be recriminates; when assailed, he turns upon his adversary with double fierceness. "I have been treated unjustly!" exclaims the wrong thinker, and then abandons himself to resentment and misery. Having no insight, and unable to distinguish evil from good, he cannot see that it is his own evil, and not his neighbour's, that is the cause of all his trouble.

The right-thinker is not concerned with thoughts about self and self-protection, and the wrong actions of others toward him cannot cause him trouble or unrest. He cannot think—"This man has wronged me." He perceives that no wrong can reach him but by his own evil deeds. He understands that his welfare is in his own hands, and thus none but himself can rob him of repose. Virtue is his protection, and retaliation is foreign to him. He holds himself steadfastly in peace, and resentment cannot enter his heart. Temptation does not find him unprepared, and it assails in vain the strong citadel of his mind. Abiding in virtue, he abides in strength and peace.

The right-thinker has discovered and acquired the right attitude of mind toward men and things— the attitude of a profound and loving repose. And this is not resignation, it is wisdom. It is not indifference, but watchful and penetrating insight. He has comprehended the facts of life; he sees things as they are. He does not overlook the particulars of life, but reads them in the light of cosmic law; sees them in their right relations as portions of the universal scheme. He sees that the universe is upheld by justice. He watches, but does not engage in, the petty quarrels and fleeting strifes of men. He cannot be a partisan. His sympathy is with all. He cannot favor one portion more than another. He knows that good will ultimatly conquer in the world, as it has conquered in individuals; that there is a sense in which good already conquers, for evil defeats itself.

Good is not defeated; justice is not set aside. Whatever man may do, justice reigns, and its eternal throne cannot be assailed and threatened, much less conquered and overthrown; and this is the source of the true thinker's abiding repose. Having become righteous, he perceives the righteous law; having acquired Love, he understands the Eternal Love; having conquered evil, he knows that good is supreme.

He only is the true thinker whose heart is free from hatred, lust, and pride; who looks out upon the world through eyes washed free from evil; whose bitterest enemy arouses no enmity, but only tender pity in his heart; who does not talk vainly about things of which he has no knowledge, and whose heart is always at peace.

And by this a man may know that his thoughts are in accordance with Truth—that there is no more bitterness in his heart, that malice has departed from him; that he loves where he formerly condemned.

A man may be learned, but if he is not wise he will not be a true thinker. Not by learning will a man triumph over evil; not by much study will he overcome sin and sorrow. Only by conquering himself will he conquer evil; only by practising righteousness will he put an end to sorrow.

Not for the clever, nor the learned, nor the self-confident is the Life Triumphant, but for the pure, the virtuous, the wise. The former achieve their particular success in life, but the latter alone achieve the Great Success, a success so invincible and complete that even an apparent defeat shines with added victory.

Virtue cannot be shaken; virtue cannot be confounded; virtue cannot be overthrown. He who thinks in accordance with virtue, who acts righteously, whose mind is the servant of Truth, he it is who conquers in life and in death; for virtue must triumph, and Righteousness and Truth are the pillars of the universe.

Calmness
and Resource

He who has Truth is always self-possessed. Hurry and excitement, anxiety and fear have no place in the purified mind and the true life. Self-conquest results in a perpetual calm. Calmness is the radiant light which adds a lustre to all the virtues. Like the nimbus round the head of a saint, it surrounds virtue with its shining halo. Without calmness a man's greatest strength is but a kind of exaggerated weakness. Where is a man's spiritual strength—where, indeed, is his ordinary manly strength—who loses his balance with almost every petty disturbance from without? And what enduring influence can a man have who forgets himself in sinful abandonment or unseemly rage in the hour of temptation and crisis?

The virtuous put a check upon themselves, and set a watch upon their passions and emotions; in this way they gain possession of the mind, and gradually acquire calmness; and, as they acquire calmness, they acquire influence, power, greatness, abiding joy, and fulness and completeness of life.

Those who do not put a check upon themselves, whose emotions and passions are their masters, who crave excitements and race after unholy pleasures—these are not yet fit for a life of joyful victory, and can neither appreciate nor receive the beautiful jewel of calmness. Such may pray for peace with their lips, but they do not desire it in their hearts; or the word "peace" may only mean to them another kind of periodic pleasure which they desire to enjoy.

In the life of calm there are no fitful periods of sinful excitement followed by reactionary hours of sorrow and remorse. There are no foolish elations followed by equal foolish depressions; no degrading actions followed by misery and loss of self-respect; but all these things are put away, and what remains is Truth, and Truth is for ever encircled with peace. The calm life is one unbroken bliss. Duties which are irksome to the ungoverned, are things of joy to the calm man; indeed, in the calm life, the word "duty" receives a new meaning; it is no longer opposed to happiness, but it is one with happiness. The calm man, the right-seeing man, cannot separate joy from duty; such separation belongs to the mind and life of the pleasure-hunter and lover of excitement.

Calmness is difficult to attain because men cling blindly to the lower disturbances of the mind for the passing pleasure which those disturbances afford. Even sorrow is sometimes selfishly gloated over as a kind of occasional luxury. But though difficult to attain, the way which leads to its attainment is simple; it consists in abandoning all those excitements and disturbances which are opposed to it, and in fortifying one's self in those steadfast virtues which do not change with changing events and circumstances, which have no violent reactions, and which therefore bestow perpetual satisfaction and abiding peace.

He only finds peace who conquers himself, who strives, day by day, after greater self-possession, greater self-control, greater calmness of mind. One can only be a joy to himself and a blessing to others in the measure that he has command of himself; and such self-command is gained only by persistent practice. A man must conquer his weaknesses by daily effort; he must understand them and study how to eliminate them from his character; and if he continues to strive, not giving way, he will gradually become victorious; and each little victory gained (though there is a sense in which no victory can be called *little*) will be so much more calmness acquired and added to his character as an eternal possession. He will thus make himself strong and capable and blessed, fit to perform his duties faultlessly, and to meet all events with an untroubled spirit. But even if he does not, in this life, reach that supreme calm which no shock can disturb, he will become sufficiently self-possessed and pure to enable him to fight the battle of life fearlessly, and to leave the world a little richer for having known the benignity of his presence.

By constantly overcoming self, a man gains a knowledge of the subtle intricacies of his mind; and it is this divine knowledge which enables him to become established in calmness. Without self-knowledge there can be no abiding peace of mind, and those who are carried away by tempestuous passions, cannot approach the holy place where calmness reigns. The weak man is like one who, having mounted a fiery steed, allows it to run away with him, and carry him withersoever it wills; the strong man is like one who, having mounted the steed, governs it with a masterly hand, and makes it go in whatever direction, and at whatever speed he commands.

Calmness is the crowning beauty of a character that has become, or is becoming, divine, and is restful and peace-giving to all who come in contact with it. Those who are still in their weakness and doubt, find the presence of the calm mind restful to their troubled minds, inspiring to their faltering feet, and rich with healing and comfort in the hour of sorrow; for he who is strong to overcome self, is strong to help others; he who has conquered soul-weariness is strong to help the weary on the way.

That calmness of mind which is not disturbed or overthrown by trials and emergencies, or by the accusations, slanders, and misrepresentations of others, is born of great spiritual strength, is the true indication of an enlightened and wise understanding. The, calm mind is the exalted mind. Divinely gentle and eternally strong, is that man who does not lose his serenity, nor forget his peace when falsehoods and indignities are heaped upon him. Such calmness is the perfect flower of self-control; it has been slowly and laboriously gained, by patiently passing through the fires of suffering, by subjecting the mind to a long process of purification.

The calm man has discovered the spring of both happiness and knowledge within himself, and it is a spring that can never run dry. His powers are at his full command, and there is no limit to his resources. In whatever direction he employs his energies, he will manifest originality and power. And this is so because he deals with things as they are, and not with mere opinions about things. If he has any opinions left, he is no longer enamoured of them, but sees them as they are—mere opinions, and therefore of no intrinsic value. He has abolished egotism, and, by obedience to law, has become one with the power in nature and the universe. His resources are untrammeled by selfishness; his energies are unhindered by pride. There is a sense in which he has ceased to regard anything as his own. Even his virtues belong to Truth, and not exclusively to his person. He has become a conscious instrument of Cosmic Power, and is no longer a mean, dwarfed thing, seeking petty personal ends. And having put away self, he has put away the greed, the misery, the troubles and fears which belong to self. He acts calmly, and accepts all consequences with equal calmness. He is efficient and accurate, and perceives all that is involved in any undertaking. He does not work blindly; he knows there is no chance of favour.

The mind of the calm man is like the surface of a still lake; it reflects life and the things of life truly. Whereas the troubled mind, like the troubled surface of a lake, gives back a distorted image of all things which fall upon it. Gazing into the serene depths within him, the self-conquered man sees a just reflection of the universe. He sees the Cosmic Perfection; sees the equity in his own lot; even those things which are regarded by the world as unjust and grievous (and which formerly appeared so to him) are now known to be the effects of his own past deeds, and are therefore joyfully accepted as portions of the perfect whole. Thus his calmness remains with him with its illimitable fund of resource in joy and enlightenment.

The calm man succeeds where the disturbed man fails. He is fitted to deal with any external difficulty, who has successfully grappled with the most intricate difficulties and problems within his own heart. He who has succeeded in governing the within, is best equipped to govern the without. The calm mind perceives a difficulty in all its bearings, and understands best how to meet it. The disturbed mind is the lost mind. It has become blind, seeing not whither to go, but *only feeling* its own unhappiness and fear. The resources of the calm man are superior to all incidents which may befall him. Nothing can alarm him, nothing can find him unprepared, nothing can shake his strong and steadfast mind. Wheresoever duty may call him, there will his strength manifest itself; there will his mind, free from the frictions of self, exhibit its silent and patient power. Whether he be engaged in things worldly or things spiritual, he will do his work with concentrated vigor and penetrating insight.

Calmness means that the mind is harmoniously adjusted, perfectly poised; all its extremes, once so antagonistic and painful, are reconciled, merged into one grand central principle with which the mind has identified itself. It means that the runaway passions are tamed and subjected, the intellect is purified, and the will is merged into the Cosmic Will; that is, it is no longer centered upon narrow personal ends, but is concerned with the good of all.

A man is not wholly victorious until he is perpetually calm. While passing things disturb him, his understanding is unripe, his heart is not altogether pure. A man cannot advance in the triumph of life while he flatters and deceives himself. He must awake, and be fully alive to the fact that his sins, sorrows, and troubles are of his own making, and belong to his own imperfect condition. He must understand that his miseries have their root in his own sins, and not in the sins of others. He must strive after calmness as the covet-ous man strives after riches; and he must not rest satisfied with any partial attainment. He will thus grow in grace and wisdom, in strength and peace, and calmness will descend upon his spirit as the refreshing dew descends upon the flowers.

Where the calm mind is, there is strength and rest, there is love and wisdom; there is one who has fought successfully innumerable battles against self, who, after long toil in secret against his own failings, has triumphed at last.

Insight
and Nobility

In the pursuit and practice of virtue, there at last comes a time when a divine insight dawns upon the mind, an insight that searches into the causes and principles of things, and which, once attained, establishes its possessor firmly in virtue, renders him invulnerable to the assaults of temptation, and invincible in his work for the world.

When the understanding is ripened by the culture of virtue, vicious inclinations disappear, and wrong-doing becomes impossible. When individual human conduct is perceived as an unbroken series of causes and effects, the perceiving mind finally decides for virtue, and the lower selfish elements are cast away for ever.

Until a man perceives the just law which operates in human life, whatever virtue he may manifest at any given time, he is not firmly established in nobility of character, he is not fully armoured with righteousness, is not safely lodged in his final refuge. Not having acquired that perfect insight which knows good and evil and which perceives the effects of all deeds both good and bad, he breaks down when assailed by temptation at those points in his character which are not well fortified, and which have, so far, dimmed his spiritual sight, and barred him from perfect vision. And by thus breaking down, he discovers that within which has hindered him, and by setting to work to remove the hindrance, he ascends still higher in the scale of virtue, and approaches nearer to that perfect insight into the true order of life which makes a man divine.

Under certain circumstances a man, held in restraint by the influence of friends, by custom and environment, and not by his own inherent purity and strength, will appear to have, and may believe himself to possess, a virtue of which he knows nothing in reality; and his lack of such virtue only appears when all outward restraints are withdrawn, and, under temptation, the concealed weakness and vice make themselves manifest.

On the other hand, the man of superior virtue will seem, in a familiar environment, to be much the same as his weaker fellows, and his virtue will not be apparent to those about him; but when he is suddenly brought in contact with great temptations or extraordinary events, his latent virtue appears in all its beauty and strength.

Insight destroys the dominion of evil, and reveals the faultless operation of the Good Law. The man of perfect insight cannot sin, because he fully understands the nature of good and evil, and it is impossible for one who knows good and evil in all their ramifications of cause and effect to choose the evil and reject the good. Just as the sane man would not choose ashes in preference to food, so the spiritually awakened man would not choose evil in preference to good. The presence of sin is an indication of self-delusion, of ignorance; the spiritual vision is warped or undeveloped, and there is confusion of mind concerning the nature of good and evil.

In the early stages of virtue, a man arrays himself against the forces of evil which appear to him to be overpowering in their might, and almost, if not entirely, unconquerable; but with the advent of insight, a new light is thrown upon the nature of things, and evil appears as it actually is—a small, dark, powerless thing, a mere negation, and not a formidable force or combination of forces. The man of insight knows that the root of evil is ignorance—and not an intelligent power—and that all sins and sufferings proceed therefrom. Thus, knowing evil to be merely deprivation of good, he cannot hate it, but manifests compassion for all sinning and suffering beings.

Indeed, be who has so far conquered the evil in his own heart as to know the nature and source of evil, cannot possibly hate, dislike, or despise any being, no matter how far removed from virtue it may be, but, while fully perceiving the degradation of character, he understands the dark spiritual condition from which such degradation springs, and so he pities and helps where, without insight, he would hate and despise. Love ever attends upon insight, and pity waits on knowledge.

That insight which proceeds, from self-purification and long acquaintance with virtue makes itself manifest in the form of *ripeness of character*, there is an unchanging strength and sweetness combined; a clearness of intellect, a virile strength of will, and a gentleness of heart—combination which denotes a cultured, mellowed, perfected being; one who has acquired sympathy, compassion, purity, and—wisdom. Thus while "Goodness gives insight," insight renders goodness permanent, fixes the mind in the love and practice of all that is pure and noble, and stamps upon man's brow the seal of divinity.

The man whose goodness is of that kind that does not alter with altered environment, or change with the changing attitudes of those around him, has reached the Divine Goodness; he understands the Supreme Good. He is no longer concerned with evil as a thing that can harm him, but he is concerned with good only; and so he ignores evil, and recognizes only good. He perceives that men commit evil out of a mistaken idea of good, and, thus perceiving, no hatred against any can enter his peaceful heart.

The life of such a man is powerful, no matter how obscure it may be, for goodness is the most powerful thing in the world, and the fact of his living and moving amongst men confers incalculable benefit upon the race, although during his lifetime, this may not be perceived and understood. So powerful is goodness that the destiny of the world was, is, and will be, in the hands of the good. The good men are the guides and emancipators of humanity. In the present period of its development, they are taking the race rapidly along in its evolutionary journey; and this, not in any mystical or miraculous sense, but in a very practical and normal sense, by their exemplary lives, by the power of their deeds. The good men who help the world are not wonder-workers, though undeveloped minds have ever tried to make them such—but the workers of righteousness, servants of the Good Law.

The world never was, is not, and will not be, under the dominion of evil, for such a condition would mean non-existence, evil being merely the negation of good, as darkness is the negation of light; and it is light, and not darkness, which is the sustaining power. Evil is the weakest thing in the world, and cannot accomplish anything. The universe not only makes for good, the universe is good, and evil always falls short and fails.

Insight is *seeing in the Light of Truth*, that Light which is the revealer of all things. As the light of day reveals all objects in the world in their proper forms, so when the Light of Truth enters the mind it reveals all the things of life in their proper proportions. He who searches his own heart by the aid of Truth, searches all hearts. He who, by long searching, has perceived the Perfect Law which is operative in his own mind, has revealed the Divine Law which is the stay and substance of the universe.

Insight disperses error and puts an end to superstition. Sin is the only error. Men attack each other's beliefs and remain in ignorance. When they get rid of their own sins they will become enlightened. Superstition springs from sin. Looking through darkened eyes, men see evil things which are delusions of ignorance; conceiving in their hearts unlawful things, their imagination is troubled with monsters and terrors which have no existence in reality. Where there is pure insight there is no fear; and devils, demons, wrathful and jealous gods, vampires and evil spirits, and all the hideous host of theological monsters, have vanished from the universe along with the feverish nightmare which gave them birth, and before the rapt gaze of the purified one there spreads a universe of orderly beauty and inviolate law.

The man of insight lives in the beatific vision of the saints, not as a fleeting experience in a moment of exceptional purity, but as a constant, normal condition of mind. He has completed his long journey through self and sorrow, and is at peace; he has conquered, and is glad. He sees all the sin and misery and pain that are in the world more plainly and vividly than other men, but he now sees it as it is in its cause, inception, growth and fruitage, and not as it appeared to him when he was blindly involved in it, and his mind was distorted by impurities. He watches the growth of beings, from the immature to the mature, through periods of change and pain, with tender compassion and solicitude, as the mother watches the growth of her child through the helpless period of its infancy.

He sees justice operating in all things. While men are waxing wrathful over the triumph of wrong, he knows that wrong has not triumphed, but is brought to naught. He sees the overruling Right which, though concealed from worldly eyes, remains forever unshaken. He sees the littleness, the puny weakness, the blind folly of evil as compared with the majesty, the invincible power, and the all-seeing wisdom of Good. And thus knowing and seeing, his mind is finally fixed in that which is good. He is devoted to Truth, and his delight is in the doing of righteousness.

When insight is born in the mind, Reality stands revealed; not a metaphysical reality distinct from the universe; not a speculative reality other than the things of life, but the. Reality of the universe itself, the Reality of " things-in-themselves." Insight is triumphant over change and decay, for it perceives the abiding in change, the eternal in the transient, the immortal in the things which pass away.

And herein is the meaning of that fixed nobility of character of the saints and sages, and, superlatively, of the Great Teachers of the Race—that they perceive and abide in Reality; they know life as it is in its completion; they understand and obey the

Righteous Law. Having conquered self, they have conquered all delusions; having triumphed over sin, they have triumphed over sorrow, having purified themselves, they see the Perfect Cosmos.

He who chooses the right, the pure, the good, and clings to them through all misunderstanding, contumely, and defeat, reaches, at last, the place of insight, and his eyes open upon the world of Truth; then his painful discipline is ended; the lower conditions no more effect him or cause him sorrow; purity and joy abide with him, and the universe again rejoices in the triumph of good, and hails another conqueror.

Man the Master

By the mastery of self, a distinct form of consciousness is evolved which would call *divine* as distinguished from that ordinary *human* consciousness which craves personal advantages and gratification on the one hand, and is involved in remorse and sorrow on the other. This divine consciousness concerns itself with humanity and the universe, with eternal verities, with righteousness, wisdom, and truth, and not with pleasures, protection, and preservation of the personality. Not that personal pleasure is destroyed, but it is no longer craved and sought, it no longer takes a foremost place; it is purified, and is received as the effect of right thought and action, and is no longer an end in itself. In divine consciousness there is neither sin nor sorrow. Even the sense of sin has passed away, and the true order and purpose of life being revealed, no cause is found for lamentation. Jesus called this state of consciousness "The Kingdom of Heaven;" Buddha named it "Nirvana;" Lao-Tze's term for it was "Tao;" Emerson refers to it as "The Over-Soul," and Dr. Bucke calls it "Cosmic Consciousness" in his valuable work bearing that title.

The ordinary human consciousness is *self-consciousness*. Self, the personality, is placed before everything else; there are ceaseless anxieties and fears concerning the self; its possible loss is thought to be the most grievous calamity, and its eternal preservation the most important thing in the universe.

In divine consciousness all this has passed away. Self has disappeared, therefore there can be no more fears and anxieties concerning the self, and things are considered and known as they are, and not as they afford pleasure or cause pain to self, not as self wishes them to be for its own temporal or eternal happiness.

The self-conscious man is subject to desire; the divinely conscious man is master of desire. The former considers what is pleasant or unpleasant; the latter acts from the righteous law without reference to pleasure or pain.

The race is passing through self-consciousness to divine consciousness; through the slavery of self, with its sense of sin and shame, to the freedom of Truth, with its sense of purity and power. The Great Teachers and Saviours of the race have already attained. In former existences they have passed through all forms of self-consciousness, and now, having subjugated self have become divinely conscious. They have reached the summit of evolution on this earth, and have no further need to be re-born in the self-conscious form. They are Masters of Life. Having conquered self, they have acquired the Supreme Knowledge. Some of them are worshipped as God because they manifest a wisdom and a consciousness which is quite distinct from the normal self-consciousness of humanity, and which is therefore regarded with, and surrounded by, incomprehensible mystery. Yet in this divine consciousness there is no mystery, but, on the contrary, a transparent simplicity which becomes apparent when the confusions of self are dispersed.

The abiding gentleness, the sublime wisdom, the perfect calm of the Great Teachers—qualities which appear supernatural when viewed from the self-conscious state—are seen to be simple and natural when the first glimmering of divine consciousness dawns in the mind; and such divine consciousness does not appear until a high degree of morality is attained by self-conscious man.

Man becomes divinely conscious, divinely wise, divinely gentle and strong in the measure that he subdues and dominates, in himself, those passions by which humanity is subdued and dominated. He only is the divine master who is master of himself. The abiding nobility, beneficent characteristics, and unobtrusive virtue which mark off the spiritually enlightened man from his fellows, are the fruits of self-conquest, the logical outcome of a long struggle to master and comprehend those mental forces which self-conscious man blindly obeys without understanding.

Self-conscious man is man the slave. He obeys his inclinations and is in submission to his passions, and to the sorrows and pains which his allegiance to those passions inflicts upon him. He is conscious of sin and sorrow, but sees no way out of these conditions; and so he invents theologies which he substitutes for effort, and which, while affording him fitful comfort through uncertain hope, leave him the easy victim of sin, and the willing subject of sorrow.

Divinely conscious man is man the master. He obeys Truth, and not self. He curbs and directs his inclinations, is conscious of a growing power over sin and sorrow, and sees that there is a way out of these conditions by the path of self-mastery. He needs no theologies to aid him, but exerts himself in right-doing, and is gladdened by a sense of victory and increasing purity and power. When his mastery is complete, he has no inclinations but those which accord with Truth; he has then become the conqueror of sin, and is no longer subject to sorrow.

Enlightened, wise and evermore peaceful and happy is he who has subjected, overcome, and cast out the turbulent self that reigned within him; the tempests of sorrow do not chill him; the cares and troubles which beset man pass him by, and no evil thing overtakes him. Secure in divine virtue, no enemy can overthrow him; no foe can do him harm. Benign and peaceful, no person, power, nor place can rob him of repose.

Man has no enemy but self, no darkness but ignorance, no suffering but that which springs from the insubordinate elements of his own nature.

No man is truly wise who is involved in likes and dislikes, wishes and regrets, desires and disappointments, sins and sorrows. All these conditions belong to the self-conscious state, and are indications of folly, weakness, and subjection.

He is truly wise who, in the midst of his worldly duties, is always calm, always gentle, always patient; who accepts things as they are, and does no wish and grieve, desire and regret. These things belong to the divinely conscious state, the dominion of Truth, and are indications of enlightenment, strength, and mastery.

He who does not desire riches, or fame, or pleasures; who enjoys what he has, yet does not lament when it is taken from him, he is indeed wise.

He who desires riches and fame, and pleasures; who is discontended with what he has, yet laments when it is taken from him, he is indeed foolish.

Man is fitted for conquest, but the conquest of territory will not avail; he must resort to the conquest of self. The conquest of territory renders man a temporal ruler, but the conquest of self makes him an eternal conqueror.

Man is destined for mastery; not the mastery of his fellow-men by force, but the mastery of his own nature by self-control. The mastery of his fellow-men by force is the crown of egotism, but the mastery of self by self-control is the crown of humility.

He is man the master who has shaken off the service of self for the service of Truth, who has established himself in the Eternal Verities. He is crowned, not only with perfect manhood, but with divine wisdom. He has overcome the disturbances of the mind and the shocks of life. He is superior to all circumstances. He is the calm spectator, but no longer the helpless tool, of events. No more a sinning, weeping, repenting mortal, he is pure, rejoicing, erect, immortal. He perceives the course of things with a glad and peaceful heart; a divine conqueror, master of life and death.

Knowledge and Victory

Faith is the beginning of the Triumphant Life, but knowledge is its consummation. Faith reveals the way, but knowledge is the goal. Faith suffers many afflictions; knowledge has transcended affliction. Faith endures; knowledge loves. Faith walks in darkness, but *believes*; knowledge acts in light, and *knows*. Faith inspires to effort; knowledge crowns effort with success. "Faith is the substance of things hoped for;" knowledge is the substance of things possessed. Faith is the helpful staff of the pilgrim; knowledge is the City of Refuge at his journey's end. Without faith there will be no knowledge, but when knowledge is acquired, the work of faith is finished.

The Life Triumphant is a life of knowledge; and by knowledge is meant, not book-learning, but life-knowing; not superficial facts committed to memory, but the deep facts and truths of life grasped and comprehended. Apart from this knowledge there is no victory for man, no rest for his weary feet, no refuge for his aching heart. There is no salvation for the foolish except by becoming wise; there is no salvation for the sinful except by becoming pure; there is no liberation for man from the turmoils and troubles of life but through divine knowledge reached by the pathway of a pure and blameless life. Nowhere is there permanent peace except in an enlightened condition of mind; and a pure life and an enlightened mind are identical.

But there *is* salvation for the foolish because wisdom can be acquired; there, is salvation for the sinful because purity can be embraced; there is liberation for all men from the troubles and turmoils of life because whosoever wills to do so—whether rich or poor, learned or unlearned—can enter the lowly way of blamelessness which leads to perfect knowledge. And because of this—that there is deliverance for the captives and victory for the defeated—there is rejoicing in the High Places, and the universe is glad.

The man of knowledge, being victorious over himself, is victorious over sin, over evil, over all the inharmonies of life. Out of the old mind marred by sin and sorrow, be has framed a new mind glorified by purity and peace. He has died out of the old world of evil, and is reborn in a new world where love and faultless law prevail, where evil is not, and he has become deathless in immortal Good.

Anxiety and fear, grief and lamentation, disappointment and regret, wretchedness and remorse—these things have no part in the world of the wise. They are the shadowy inhabitants of the world of self, and cannot live, nay, they are seen to have no substantiality—in the light of wisdom. The dark things of life are the dark conditions of a mind not yet illuminated by the light of wisdom. They follow self as the shadow the substance. Where selfish desires go, there they follow; where sin is, there they are.

There is no rest in self; there is no light in self, and where the flames of turbulent passions and the fires of consuming desires are rife, the cool airs of wisdom and peace are not felt.

Safety and assurance, happiness and repose, satisfaction and contentment, joy and peace—these are the abiding possessions of the wise, earned by right of self-conquest, the results of righteousness, the wages of a blameless life.

The substance of a right life is enlightenment (knowledge), and the spirit of knowledge is peace.

To be victorious over self in all the issues of life is to know life as it is in reality, and not as it appears in the nightmare of self; it is to be in peace in all passages, and not to be stricken with trouble and grief in the common happenings of life.

As the ripe scholar is no more troubled by incorrect work and lessons imperfectly done, and the painful reproof and punishment formerly inflicted by his teachers are left behind forever, so the perfected scholar in virtue, the wise man, the enlightened doer of righteousness, is no more troubled with wrong-doing and folly (which are merely the imperfectly accomplished lessons of life), and the scourgings of sorrow and remorse have passed away forever.

The skilled scholar has no more doubt or fear concerning his ability. He has overcome and dispersed the ignorance of his intellect. He has attained to learning, and he knows that he has attained; and he so knows because, having undergone innumerable intellectual tests in the form of lessons and examinations, he has at last proved his skill by passing successfully through the severest tests of scholarship. And now he no longer fears, but rejoices when severe tests are applied to prove his ability. He is capable, confident, and glad.

Even so the skilled doer of righteousness is no more troubled with doubt and fear concerning his

destiny. He has overcome and dispersed the ignorance of his heart. He has attained to wisdom, and
he *knows* that he has attained; and he so knows
because where he formerly failed and fell when
tested by the wrong conduct of others, he now
maintains his patience and calmness under the
severest tests of accusation and reproof.

Herein is the glory and victory of divine knowledge, that, understanding the nature of deeds both
good and bad, the enlightened doer of good deeds
no longer suffers through the bad deeds of others.
Their actions towards him can never cause him
pain and sorrow, nor rob him of his peace. Having taken refuge in good, evil can no more reach
or harm him. He returns good for evil, and over-
comes the weakness of evil by the power of good.

The man who is involved in bad deeds imagines that the bad deeds of others are powerful to do
him injury, are filled with grievious harm against
him, and he is stung with pain and overwhelmed
with sorrow, not for his own bad deeds (for these
be does not see) but for the wrong deeds of others.
Involved in ignorance, he has no spiritual strength,
no refuge, and no abiding peace.

The man victorious over self is the true seer; not
the seer of spirits or supernatural phenomena, for
such seeing is narrow and illusory, but the seer of
life as it is, both in its particular aspects and in its

divine principles; the seer of the spiritual universe, of cosmic law, cosmic love, and cosmic liberty.

The man of knowledge and victory, who has shaken off the painful dreams of self, has awakened with a new vision which beholds a new and glorified universe. He is the seer of the Eternal, and is blessed with perfect love and endless peace. He is lifted far above all sordid desires, narrow aims, and selfish love and hate; and being so lifted up he perceives the lawful course of things, and does not grieve when overtaken by the inevitable. He is above the world of sorrow, not because he has become cold and cruel, but because he abides, in a love where no thought of self can enter, and where the well-being of others is all-in-all. He is sorrowless because he is selfless. He is serene because he knows that whatever he receives, it is good, and whatever is taken from him, that also is good. He has transmuted sorrow into love, and is filled with Infinite tenderness and abounding compassion. His power is not violent, ambitious, worldly, but pure, peaceful, heavenly, and he is possessed of a hidden strength which knows how to stand and when to bend for the good of others and the world. He is a Teacher, though he speak but little; he is a Master, yet he has no desire to rule others; he is a Conqueror, but makes no attempt to subdue his fellowmen. He has become a conscious instrument for the outworking of cosmic law, and is an intelligent, enlightened power directing the evolution of the Race.

At this, the beginning of a new epoch, let the Good News again go forth throughout the world that there is purity for the sinful, comfort for the afflicted, healing for the broken-hearted, and triumph for the defeated. In your heart, O man! stained as it is with sin, and torn with conflicting desires, there is a place of power, a citadel of strength; you are the dwelling-place of the Supreme Good, and the Sceptre of Victory awaits you: deep in your consciousness is the High Seat of Empire. Arise O stricken one! ascend your kingly throne.

James Allen: A Memoir

By Lily L. Allen

from *The Epoch* (February–March 1912)

> *Unto pure devotion*
> *Devote thyself: with perfect meditation*
> *Comes perfect act, and the right-hearted rise—*
> *More certainly because they seek no gain—*
> *Forth from the bands of body, step by step.*
> *To highest seats of bliss.*

James Allen was born in Leicester, England, on November 28th, 1864. His father, at one time a very prosperous manufacturer, was especially fond of "Jim," and before great financial failures overtook him, he would often look at the delicate, refined boy, poring over his books, and would say, "My boy, I'll make a scholar of you."

The Father was a high type of man intellectually, and a great reader, so could appreciate the evident thirst for education and knowledge which he observed in his quiet studious boy.

As a young child he was very delicate and nervous, often suffering untold agony during his school days through the misunderstanding harshness of some of his school teachers, and others with whom he was forced to associate, though he retained always the tenderest memories of others—one or two of his teachers in particular, who no doubt are still living.

He loved to get alone with his books, and many a time he has drawn a vivid picture for me, of the hours he spent with his precious books in his favourite corner by the home fire; his father, whom he dearly loved, in his arm chair opposite also deeply engrossed in his favourite authors. On such evenings he would question his father on some of the profound thoughts that surged through his soul—thoughts he could scarcely form into words—and the father, unable to answer, would gaze at him long over his spectacles, and at last say: "My boy, my boy, you have lived before"—and when the boy eagerly but reverently would suggest an answer to his own question, the father would grow silent and thoughtful, as though he *sensed* the future man and his mission, as he looked at the boy and listened to his words—and many a time he was heard to remark, "Such knowledge comes not in one short life."

There were times when the boy startled those about him into a deep concern for his health, and they would beg him not to *think so much*, and in after years he often smiled when he recalled how his father would say—"Jim, we will have you in the Churchyard soon, if you think so much."

Not that he was by any means unlike other boys where games were concerned. He could play leap-frog and marbles with the best of them, and those who knew him as a man—those who were privileged to meet him at "Bryngoleu"—will remember how he could enter into a game with all his heart. Badminton he delighted in during the summer evenings, or whenever he felt he could.

About three years after our marriage, when our little Nora was about eighteen months old, and he about thirty-three, I realized a great change coming over him, and knew that he was renouncing everything that most men hold dear that he might find Truth, and lead the weary sin-stricken world to Peace. He at that time commenced the practice of rising early in the morning, at times long before daylight, that he might go out on the hills—like One of old—to commune with God, and meditate on Divine things. I do not claim to have understood him fully in those days. The light in which he lived and moved was far too white for my earth-bound eyes to see, and a *sense of it only* was beginning to dawn upon me. But I knew I dare not stay him or hold him back, though at times my woman's heart cried out to do so, waiting him all my own, and not then understanding his divine mission.

Then came his first book, "From Poverty to Power." This book is considered by many his best book. It has passed into many editions, and tens of thousands have been sold all over the world, both authorized and pirated editions, for perhaps no author's works have been more pirated than those of James Allen.

As a private secretary he worked from 9 a.m. to 6 p.m., and used every moment out of office writing his books. Soon after the publication of "From Poverty to Power" came "All These Things Added," and then "As a Man Thinketh," a book perhaps better known and more widely read than any other from his pen.

About this time, too, the "Light of Reason" was founded and he gave up all his time to the work of editing the Magazine, at the same time carrying on a voluminous correspondence with searchers after Truth all over the world. And ever as the years went by he kept straight on, and never once looked back or swerved from the path of holiness. Oh, it was a blessed thing indeed to be the chosen one to walk by the side of his earthly body, and to watch the glory dawning upon him!

He took a keen interest in many scientific subjects, and always eagerly read the latest discovery in astronomy, and he delighted in geology and botany. Among his favourite books I find Shakespeare, Milton, Emerson, Browning, The Bhagavad-Gita, the Tao-Tea-King of Lao-Tze, the Light of Asia, the Gospel of Buddha, Walt Whitman, Dr. Bucke's Cosmic Consciousness, and the Holy Bible.

He might have written on a wide range of subjects had he chosen to do so, and was often asked for articles on many questions outside his particular work, but he refused to comply, consecrating his whole thought and effort to preach the Gospel of Peace.

When physical suffering overtook him he never once complained, but grandly and patiently bore his pain, hiding it from those around him, and only we who knew and loved him so well, and his kind, tender Doctor, knew how greatly he suffered. And yet he stayed not; still he rose before the dawn to meditate, and commune with God; still he sat at his desk and wrote those words of Light and Life which will ring down through the ages, calling men and women from their sins and sorrows to peace and rest.

Always strong in his complete manhood, though small of stature physically, and as gentle as he was strong, no one ever heard an angry word from those kind lips. Those who served him adored him; those who had business dealings with him trusted and honoured him. Ah! how much my heart prompts me to write of his self-sacrificing life, his tender words, his gentle deeds, his knowledge and his wisdom. But why? Surely there is no need, for do not his books speak in words written by his own hand, and will they not speak to generations yet to come?

About Christmas time I saw the change coming, and understood it not—blind! blind! blind! I could not think it possible that *he* should be taken and *I* left.

But we three—as if we knew—clung closer to each other, and loved one another with a greater love—if that were possible—than ever before. Look at his portrait given with the January "Epoch," and reproduced again in this, and you will see that even then our Beloved, our Teacher and Guide, was letting go his hold on the physical. He was leaving us then, and we didn't know it. Often I had urged him to stop work awhile and rest, but he always gave me the same answer, "My darling, when I stop I must go, don't try to stay my hand."

And so he worked on, until that day, Friday, January 12, 1912, when, about one o'clock he sat down in his chair, and looking at me with a great compassion and yearning in those blessed eyes, he cried out, as he stretched out his arms to me, *"Oh, I have finished, I have finished, I can go no further, I have done."*

Need I say that everything that human aid and human skill could do was done to keep him still with us. Of those last few days I dare scarcely write. How could my pen describe them? And when we knew the end was near, with his dear hands upon my head in blessing, he gave his work and his beloved people into my hands, charging me to bless and help them, until I received the call to give up my stewardship!

"I will help you," he said, "and if I can I shall come to you and be with you often."

Words, blessed words of love and comfort, *for my heart alone* often came from his lips, and a sweet smile ever came over the pale calm face when our little Nora came to kiss him and speak loving words to him, while always the gentle voice breathed the tender words to her—*"My little darling!"*

So calmly, peacefully, quietly, he passed from us at the dawn on Wednesday, January 24, 1912. "Passed from us," did I say? Nay, only the outer garment has passed from our mortal vision. He lives! and when the great grief that tears our hearts at the separation is calmed and stilled, I think that we shall know that he is still with us. We shall again rejoice in his companionship and presence.

When his voice was growing faint and low, I heard him whispering, and leaning down to catch the words I heard—"At last, at last—at home—my wanderings are over"—and then, I heard no more, for my heart was breaking within me, and I felt, for *him* indeed it was *"Home at last!"* but for me—And then, as though he knew my thoughts, he turned and again holding out his hands to me, he said: "I have only one thing more to say to you, my beloved, and that is I love you, and I will be waiting for you; good-bye."

I write this memoir for those who love him, for those who will read it with tender loving hearts, and tearful eyes; for those who will not look critically at the way in which I have tried to tell out of my lonely heart this short story of his life and passing away—for *his* pupils, and, therefore, my friends.

We clothed the mortal remains in *pure white linen*, symbol of his fair, pure life, and so, clasping the photo of the one he loved best upon his bosom—they committed all that remained to the funeral pyre.

About the Author

James Allen was one of the pioneering figures of the self-help movement and modern inspirational thought. A philosophical writer and poet, he is best known for his book *As a Man Thinketh*. Writing about complex subjects such as faith, destiny, love, patience, and religion, he had the unique ability to explain them in a way that is simple and easy to comprehend. He often wrote about cause and effect, as well as overcoming sadness, sorrow and grief.

Allen was born in 1864 in Leicester, England into a working-class family. His father travelled alone to America to find work, but was murdered within days of arriving. With the family now facing economic disaster, Allen, at age 15, was forced to leave school and find work to support them.

During stints as a private secretary and stationer, he found that he could showcase his spiritual and social interests in journalism by writing for the magazine *The Herald of the Golden Age.*

In 1901, when he was 37, Allen published his first book, *From Poverty to Power.* In 1902 he began to publish his own spiritual magazine, *The Light of Reason* (which would be retitled *The Epoch* after his death). Each issue contained announcements, an editorial written by Allen on a different subject each month, and many articles, poems, and quotes written by popular authors of the day and even local, unheard of authors.

His third and most famous book *As a Man Thinketh* was published in 1903. The book's minor popularity enabled him to quit his secretarial work and pursue his writing and editing career full time. He wrote 19 books in all, publishing at least one per year while continuing to publish his magazine, until his death. Allen wrote when he had a message—one that he had lived out in his own life and knew that it was good.

In 1905, Allen organized his magazine subscribers into groups (called "The Brotherhood") that would meet regularly and reported on their meetings each month in the magazine. Allen and his wife, Lily Louisa Oram, whom he had married in 1895, would often travel to these group meetings to give speeches and read articles. Some of Allen's favorite writings, and those he quoted often, include the works of Shakespeare, Milton, Emerson, the Bible, Buddha, Whitman, Trine, and Lao-Tze.

Allen died in 1912 at the age of 47. Following his death, Lily, with the help of their daughter, Nora took over the editing of *The Light of Reason*, now under the name *The Epoch*. Lily continued to publish the magazine until her failing eyesight prevented her from doing so. Lily's life was devoted to spreading the works of her husband until her death at age 84.

Printed in the USA
CPSIA information can be obtained
at www.ICGtesting.com
JSHW012042140824
68134JS00033B/3205

9 781722 502430